TABLE OF CONTENTS:

The Story Quilt
Bionic Mama
Mama's Poem
My Daddy
The Ageless One
Grandpa Doesn't Know Me
Be a Child
Childhood
My Child
Christmas Memories 1087
The Box Bed
Six Cousins
Terms of Existence
Memories
Right vs. Wrong
The First Step
Dawn
The Storm
Living
Hawaiian Morning
Titanic
A Rainbowl
Morning
The Events of Dreams
Today, Tomorrow, and Yesterday
Burglar in Our Attic
Too Middle Class
Happiness
Silent Statues
Respect
In Charge of Happiness
Feelings
Dream Catcher
The Buffalo: Bison Bison
Beauty on the Land
Castles
The Owl and the Hawk
Ancient Tree
The Challenger Seven
The Columbia Seven
Endeavour: The Dream
The Chain of Islands
Homeless in Hawai'i
The Minstrel on the Shore
Poor Man
Angels in April

Perfection
Revising
The Game Plan
Out of the Blue
Recipes
Checked Gift
Comet capers
March 20, 1961
Worth of Things
Retirement
Hijacked
The Jaunt
The Palatte Parade
Colorful Tricks
Twenty-Twenty
The Soul
Life
Skeleton in the Closet
My Jesus Isn't a Republican
Dear World
Secret Places
Wolves vs. Man
Sin City
Polluted Water
Tessalated Birds
Be Cereus
Hexadragon
Which?
Travels
Election Day
Congressmen
Corporate Patsy
Trapped By Fear
Unwanted
Wasted Treasures
Elected Woes
The Power of One
The Legacy
Capitol City
The Chronical of 45
Pride
Freedom is not Free
Pathways and Memories
It's Time!
My Prayer

MEMORIES, EVENTS, & THOUGHTS

WRITTEN & ILLUSTRATED BY
CAROLYN MACY
PHOTOGRAPHY BY
JEREMY MACY

Dedicated to my family, and friends.

Memories, Events, & Thoughts
Copyright©2020 by Carolyn Macy and
Jeremy Macy. All rights reserved.'

No part of this publication may be reproduced, stored in retrieval system or transmitted in any way by any means, electronic, mechanical, photocopy, recording or otherwise without the prior permission of the author except as provided by USA copyright law.

Library of Congress Control Number: 2020911682

Published by Carolyn Macy
6227 81st Ave. N.E. | Norman, Oklahoma 73026 USA
405.401.2012

Book design copyright (c) 2020 by Carolyn Macy.
Written and Illustrated by Carolyn Macy.
Photography by Jeremy Macy.

Published in the United States of America
ISBN: 978-1-7328604-4-5 softcover
Anthology: Poetry. Photography.

THE STORY QUILT

June 7, 2009

This quilt tells a story
  Of tee-shirt souvenirs,
Bought in places I've traveled
  During growing-up years.

Grandmother and I cut
  From each tee-shirt a square
And arranged it with others
  Through much thoughtful care.

She sewed them together,
  Those pieces for me.
Though this project was trying,
  She worked lovingly.

Each square gives a moment,
  That with others do make
A patchwork of memories
  In a quilted keepsake.

From tee-shirts outgrown
  And combined in this measure,
My grandmother's skill
  Made this quilt a prized treasure.

BIONIC MAMA
December 2, 2004

She's my bionic mama
With both her knees replaced.
Good women like her you can't keep down
Once both her shoes are laced.

She's my bionic mama
When her dentures once are in.
She's eating better than before,
For she's eating once again.

She's my bionic mama
With her glasses on her face.
She now can see so perfectly
And spots things out of place.

She's my bionic mama
With her hip the next in need.
A replacement neatly fixed it;
Now she's walking in the lead.

What is next we do not wonder. . .
There's always something next in trauma.
She'll get it fixed, and then she's off. . .
She's our bionic mama!

MAMA'S POEM
January 8-12, 2012

She was our solid rock
As lasting as the sun,
Renowned for living right,
And friend to everyone.

"Thanks for calling." And "Good night."
These words of last farewell,
Last word she spoke to me
Before her parting knell.

In Heaven there's a glow
That wasn't there before.
Our Father called her home
And opened wide his door.

She traveled onward, upward
As her soul took solo flight,
To leave behind her loved ones
As darkness turned to light.

She joined the hosts above,
Who ascended prior to date,
To be united once again
Inside the Heaven's gate.

Secure and safe forever,
With Daddy by her side,
She waits for those she left behind
To cross the veiled divide.

Estel Sarajane Porter Little
August 20, 1017--December 23, 2011

MY DADDY
November 30, 2004

My daddy walked on in the summer
To his heavenly spot in the skies,
I shall miss his sly smile and the twinkle
Held there in his grayish-blue eyes.

There's a spot in my heart that is missing
That forever has been there for me.
And his absence grows more overwhelming:
For I'm missing that one I can't see.

My daddy can look down upon me
From his chair sitting high in the sky,
And it's true though that now I do miss him,
I shall see him again bye and bye.

John Russel Little
September 8, 1912 - July 14, 2004

THE AGELESS ONE
April 13, 1961

The ageless one sat beneath the tree
  In its welcoming shade to doze
As the hours drug by--from morn to eve--
  Waiting for day to close.
His eyes had dimmed from advancing years
  And his raven hair turned white,
And he carried a cane in his withered hand
  For his step was no longer light.
The years had sped for a century--save one--
  From the boyhood days of his youth
When he was the finest of all the young men
  And renown for his bravery and truth.
Then slowly his friends began leaving this world,
  But his life still lingered on.
Now he is the last of all his old friends
  With memories of times that are gone.

GRANDPA DOESN'T KNOW ME!
July 27, 2010

Grandpa doesn't seem to know me!
Mama tells me that is so.
We used to laugh and play together;
He's not the one I used to know.

Grandpa doesn't know me now.
Mama says it's just his way.
He still remembers many things
To tell about his yesterday.

Grandpa gets real mad at me.
Mama says he loves me still
But cannot keep his temper down;
It's just that Grandpa now is ill.

My grandpa sits and stares as
Mama speaks of things he knew,
And this is what I say to Mama,
"I'll always love my grandpa too!"

BE A CHILD
November 9, 1991

You're a child for just once little girl, little guy.
Be a child while you can, quickly life passes by.
Just a while does it last and you cannot return.
Grown-up is forever, which time lets you earn.

Now dream all your dreams and do all of your play
For childhood is but a short step on your way.
It's the eve in your life and you have much to learn.
You're a child only once and the seasons will turn.

Time waits for no one and it hurries on by.
Grown-up is forever and childhood a sigh.
You'll grow-up too fast, so as long as you can
Be a child, for you'll soon be a woman or man.

CHILDHOOD
March 24, 2009

Our journey through childhood
Is special though swift.
Those memories we made,
Makes our childhood our gift.

Memories affect us
In ways unaware,
With things that we love,
Or things we must bear.

To this very day
From the long ago past,
There are things in my mind
That remain and will last.

Sometimes a memory
Or event I forgot,
Is spurred by the moment
And recalled into thought.

One of those things
In my memory's clear view,
Was when a wild leopard
Escaped from our zoo.

After that happened,
My fancy roamed wild
At his prowling around
When I was a child.

His escape was short lived
When his hunger won out,
He returned to the zoo
From his wandering route.

But still to this day,
The shadows of night
Make forms in the darkness
That move in my sight.

MY CHILD
August 19, 2010

My Child,

I cannot dream your dreams for you,
Or make my dreams through you come true,
But maybe I will plant that seed
That helps to grow the dream you need.
You cannot live on laurels past
For things will change--they do not last.
What you become and what you do
Depends upon what's best for you!

Self-styled!

CHRISTMAS MEMORIES 1987

January 6, 2014

The lights went out when our
Electric lines came down,
And after sunset passed,
Deep darkness veiled our town.

Our water only dripped;
A candle offered light.
We made a blanket tent
That kept us warm that night.

We opened gifts next day
Around an unlit tree,
For Santa found our house
And made delivery.

With roads too slick to drive
And weather much too cold,
We stayed at home instead
For Christmas to unfold.

A kerosene fueled stove
We used to give us heat
And cooked our meals upon
When it came time to eat.

With all our power gone,
We placed our food outdoor
Where chilly winter cold
Would keep it safe to store.

Outside the gauge froze firm
Upon this holiday,
But inside we kept warm
And whiled our time away.

We played with toys and games
Received that Christmas Day,
Then wrapped ourselves up well
To go outside and play.

We sledded down our drive
And played out in the cold,
A winter wonderland
Uncommon to behold.

Some bending branches snapped,
Then crashed down to the ground.
We played in places where
Those trees did not surround.

Our home's electric works
Proved useless to exist,
But of our fondest Christmases,
This one still tops our list.

THE BOX BED
November 18, 2009

A tiny space to hold a lot
And store her treasured stuff.
She stacked the boxes triple deep
To make the space enough.

She stacked the boxes three across
With four more rows to add.
Upon the box arrangement,
She placed a mattress pad.

Next came pillows and the sheets
And followed with a spread.
A place to sleep she needed.
These boxes made her bed!

SIX COUSINS
June 27, 2020

Sunshine and summertime,
Six cousins outside
Finding things to do
And keeping occupied.

TERMS OF EXISTENCE
January 20, 2010

Love: the height of one's soul.
Hate: the Devil's prized goal.
Challenge: one's spirit delight.
Success: when a challenge's done right.
Accomplish: a time to sing and shout.
Learning: what life is all about.
Ignorance: a lack of knowledge therein.
Defeat: a chance to try again.
Snobbery: contempt of one's peers.
Old Age: a gift of more years.

MEMORIES
September 29, 2013

The things we did
Our knowledge learned
Those battle fought
And treasures earned.

Some magic moments
Brought tears of joy
That tragic times
Did not destroy.

The games we played,
Long bridges crossed,
Good friends we made
Some treasures lost.

When all is done
And all is said,
It formed the life
That we have led.

RIGHT VS WRONG
March 31, 2018

Something right is never wrong
Doing right can make you strong
Righting wrongs make powerful play
Creating for a better day.

A wrong is never right,
Be it hidden or in sight.
Changes slowly come along
So try to keep from doing wrong.

February 18, 2012

We try to learn from living
The things that's right to do.
Right comes from lessons learned before
That guides us safely through.

It may not make you wonderful,
Nor even make you wise.
By doing something right at first
Will bring a treasure in disguise.

There's no right way to do a wrong
Or make a wrong a right.
When something's wrong, it's wrong.
Make that your guiding light.

A wrong takes time, a wrong is wrong.
What satisfaction does it bring?
It takes hard work to solve a wrong,
So try for doing right each thing.

When something's wrong, just stop
To think and sort things through.
Again, then start with what you know
And make it right for you.

It may take time, but try for right
When you begin a deed.
It might be hard, it might be slow,
But it comes when you succeed!

THE FIRST STEP
February 5, 1992

The hardest step is first,
So some will never start
To do some untried task
That takes a daring heart....

Unsure to make a choice,
Uncertain, lags behind,
Afraid to see it through...
So goes their state of mind.

Does the fear of trying
Stop them from what they'll get,
Or their fear of failure
Make easier to quit?

A second time they slow
That step that should begin,
But caution makes them pause
And fail to step again.

Once more they stop to lose
Whatever could have been.
They needed one first step--
The hardest to begin.

Photos by Jeremy Macy
Poetry by Carolyn Macy
©May2011

DAWN
October 22, 1991

Softly breathing, whispering;
Pink, then orange to yellow, then blue,
As softly, oh so softly
Tiptoeing through the changing hue.
Touching stilled-forms oh so gently,
Warming diamond, sparkling dew.
Waking creatures from their slumber,
Misty visions brought to view.

THE STORM
September 15, 2005

Streaking fingers in the night
Make the darken heavens bright
With crecendos rumbling thunder
In celestrial, symphonic wonder.
Darkened clouds, they build and lower
Encircling currents rip and roar.
Icy spheres crash to the ground,
Shread and tear; then bounce around;
Eternal moments engulfed in sound.
Refreshing moisture clearing air,
Gives magic quietness--everywhere.

LIVING
September 30, 2009

Do your best.
Live without greed.
Share what you can.
Help those in need.

Behave fairly.
Have trust above.
Be true to self
And those you love.

Smile with laughter.
Sing and be glad.
Look for the good
When times turn bad.

Dare to dream.
Dare to do.
Have no regrets
When life is through.

HAWAIIAN MORNING
December 3, 2004

Oh the morning is delightful
When you're on a sandy beach
And the sun beats warmly on you
With cool breezes in your reach.
The palm trees sway so graceful
And the bird songs fill the air,
While the ocean roars in rhythm
As a rainbow hovers there!

THE TITANIC
1959-1960

Behold the proud Titanic;
The "Lady of the Sea"...
Aboard the rich and fashionable
Partied festively.

Unsinkable she claimed to be.
She had no care nor fear.
She scoffed at floating dangers
That sometimes came quite near.

Suddenly a jagged peak
Appeared within her path.
It struck the bold unsinkable
Unleashing sudden wrath.

The night was cold and dark.
Her decks began to list.
She sent out calls of S.O.S.
For help to come assist.

Not far away in ignorance
The California steamed.
Her wireless closed down for the night,
Though far her lights were beamed.

The proud Titanic saw them.
Distress was growing great.
Her people clambored lifeboats
While Titanic waited fate.

Then listing steeply in the water,
Slowly she submerged to lay
Across the sands beneath the waves,
Forever there to stay.

A RAINBOW
July 12, 2004

Everyday a rainbow
Appears for us to see.
The sun shines bright in azure skies,
And liquid sunshine falls on me.

Its pot of gold is in my reach,
But yet so far away.
But when I step to touch it,
It never seems to stay.

With each new step I take,
It stays beyond my reach.
Yet with its charm it leads me on
Along the sandy beach.

MORNING
June 9, 1987

The earth was kissed with lips of dew
Awakened from its sleep,
With softness from beginning light
Caressing eyes to take a peep.
The smell of freshness on the breath
That breezes gently blow
To bring the ecstacy of dawn,
Which lingers briefly all aglow.

THE EVENTS OF DREAMS: 1986

April 23, 1987

A whisp of brightness in the night,
A bit of conquered soul delight,
A dream of childhood dawned at night--
Halley's Comet.

A cloud of smoke hung in the air,
A shattered ship with seven there,
A rain of dreams for those who dare--
The Challenger.

A mighty ship beneath the sea,
A unique vessel, doomed was she,
A pictured dream discovery--
The Titanic.

Family trip, Space Center scene,
Disney World and St. Augustine,
A tour of states, an ocean seen---
Florida Trip.

Today, Tomorrow, and Yesterday
July 7, 2011-October 14, 2012

Today begins the future
As it also leaves the past:
A time for making memories--
For that is what will last.

Today's a time to plan,
To choose your path and goal.
Quit fretting over losses
That's out of your control.

Today is gained or lost
Depending on your drive.
With heart and sweat your gusto
Will keep your goal alive.

BURGLAR IN OUR ATTIC
March 11, 2006

There's a burglar that visits our attic
With some bumps and some bangs in the night.
It starts as the sun is just setting
In the eve of the dimming twilight.

A trap we then set in its pathway
That burglar did travel each eve.
When morning arrived we all saw it,
Entrapped with no hope for reprieve.

No longer an attic eve burglar,
It fussed and it fumed at our sight.
We released our masked friend in the deep woods
Away from our attic at night.

TOO MIDDLE CLASS
April 25, 2007

Trapped in the middle;
  Squeezed from each side
With no way to be rescued;
  No places to hide.
Too taxed for the wages;
  Displaced in the job.
Cheap labor replaces;
  Outsourcing plays hob.
Too right to be left;
  Too left to be right.
Too weak to have clout
  To champion the fight.
Too old to be young;
  Too young to be old.
Too much in the middle
  To fit out of the mold.
Too poor to be rich;
  Too rich to be poor.
What's needed just misses
  To make things secure.
Too schooled to be dumb;
  Too dumb to be smart.
Too fast to be slow;
  Too slow from the start.
Too much and too little;
  Too little to count.
Trapped in the middle...
  That midmost amount!

HAPPINESS
May 15, 2005

The route of life is short
And filled with many choices.
Choose the best of those you can
So that your life rejoices.

Enjoy each shining moment
That comes along your way.
For only once you have it,
Then it shifts to yesterday.

What we have done is past.
We can't undo the deed.
We hopefully will learn
To do just what we need.

Take your milestones as they come,
And master each in stride...
Those treasures and those trials
That do in life abide.

To know that you're in charge
Of happiness that's yours,
That you empower your happiness,
And choose if it endures.

Happiness will mean forgiveness
Of those who do you wrong.
To get all things done right,
It takes your whole life long.

Silent statues in the night
Seen by moon's reflected light.
A cutting cadence breezes blow,
To sweep the grasslands golden glow.

RESPECT
December 22, 2004

You can't buy respect:
It can only be earned
By doing what's right
For all those concerned.
Your credibility
Is also in play
To do your best:
To do what you say.

You can't buy respect,
But it's certainly not free.
It demands working hard
For that which must be.
You can't buy respect,
It's an honor you earn
From people who know you
And gift back in return.

IN CHARGE OF HAPPINESS
April 4, 2005

I'm in charge of happiness.
Happiness is up to me.
Keep lips curved up, not down...
Having smiles and not a frown
Makes happiness happen to be.

Smiles make the longest impressions,
And happiness comes from the smiles
Allowing our spirits to be
Loving and caring and free
Along life's highway of trials.

FEELINGS
January 3, 2005

Broken bones are soon repaired
And function as before.
A broken soul has lost a part
That's lost forevermore.

Accusing words untrue
Can sear the soul within.
A hasty word misspoken
Can stop what might have been.

Great volumes actions speak
Like hasty words unthought.
A woeful soul can hide from sight
What hurt these actions brought.

Please don't dwell upon mistakes
That were not meant to be.
It's not a perfect world
To have such harmony.

So when you're feeling bad
About how things should be,
Don't diminish one's respect
By speaking hastily.

DREAM CATCHER

A circled web
By window site
Just made for dreams
That come at night:
To catch and keep
Bad dreams from you,
While letting good ones
Flutter through.

The Buffalo: Bison bison

Witchita Mountains, Oklahoma

They made the prairies thunder
As they moved from place to place.
They lived in herds of thousands
Ranging miles for grazing space.

They were the store of yesteryears
That plainsmen valued and pursued.
They gave him fuel for heat and warmth,
And clothing, shelter, tools, and food.

She used her brush and pallette
To paint some beauty on the land,
The sky, the trees, the houses,
And with her Master's hand…

Castles

There are many kinds of castles
Which people choose to build,
But castles built within
Are better ones fulfilled.

THE OWL AND THE HAWK

An owl and a hawk
Sat in neighboring trees
On limbs gently swaying
From late summer breeze.

Unhappy of sharing
These parts close about,
They looked at each other
With feathers puffed out.

A movement they saw
As they looked toward the ground,
Then each dove to catch it
With scarcely a sound.

As things tend to happen,
They saw only one thing,
Forgetting each other
As each took to wing.

Their paths came together
To mask that in sight
And causing each other
To falter in flight.

But all was not lost
For another's sharp eyes
Saw and swooped down
To fly off with their prize.

Knarled and dark
   it quietly rose
Among the
   granite boulders.
No leaves did hide
   the clouded sky
That wrapped its
   Ancient shoulders.

THE CHALLENGER SEVEN
March 1986
(Occurred on January 28, 1986)

A silent liftoff
In the early morning light...
Followed by its roar.

Like knights of old their glory was there;
The burning sun, the spacious air,
Desires to conquer with love to know
Adventure, triumph, heartbreak, woe.
The metal armor grandly worn,
Sometimes it fails; it's rent and torn.
The spirit left remains unscathed
To fly unto a hero's grave;
Transcended, solemn, reverence shown
For seven heroes challenged--flown.

THE COLUMBIA SEVEN
(Occurred on February 1, 2003)

Again a seven returned to fly
Into the heavens across the sky,
Their ship ablaze and streaking down,
To scatter near a Texas town.

I cried then as I do now
In tremendous sorrow my head I bow:
Columbia and Challenger, now and then seven
Streaking across an azure heaven.

ENDEAVOUR: THE DREAM
May 16, 2011

We watched her lift her nose in flight
Above her trail of fire and smoke;
A gleaming white from solar shine
As early morning skies awoke.

In awe we stood and held our breath.
Our spirits soared with her in flight.
We lived our dream to see her rise
From launching pad towards orbit height.

HOMELESS IN HAWAI'I
April 11, 2005

I'm homeless in Hawai'i
As lucky as can be.
I'm living there in Paradise
Where rent for me is free.

My swimming pool is mighty.
(I swim the restless sea.)
There showers on the beach
Wash sand and salt from me.

The sky's my azure ceiling
Which has two lamps for lights
That by themselves turn on with
Sunny days and moonlit nights.

The sandy beach provides my bed
Beneath a swaying tree
Blown gently by prevailing winds
To cool the night for me.

I work by day to fill my needs,
Yet I'm a homeless guy.
I can't afford the cost of home
Because it's much too high.

I'm homeless in Hawai'i,
And happy as can be.
I'm living there in Paradise
Beside the restless sea.

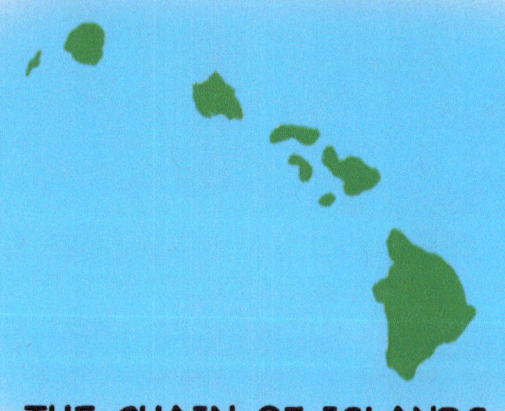

THE CHAIN OF ISLANDS
November 14, 2009

An ocean chain of islands
Began quite long ago
On the ocean bottom
In a fiery glow.

As time passed by,
Each peaked above the swells
With lava showers glowing,
Growing up in spells.

Each took their turn
Upon the molten spot,
Riding on the ocean floor
To move on as they ought.

This happened many times
To make the chain we know,
And even now it makes
A future island grow.

BLAYZE, THE MINSTREL ON THE SHORE

June 28, 2008

The minstrel sat
   On the shore by the sea
Strumming on his guitar
   A soft melody.
For all who strolled by,
   For those who could hear,
He played from the heart
   Refrains sweet to the ear.
Day in and day out
   This minstrel, he played.

Carried on the sea breezes
   Swirled the music he made.
He nodded "Hello!"
   To familiar faces;
People he met
   From so many places.
He followed his dream
   In search of the door
That would take him in
   As he played on the shore.

POOR MAN

September 5, 2005
(After Hurricane Katrina hit New Orleans August 29, 2005)

Let the strong winds blow pushing everything down,
And the cold, storm waters flood the streets of town.
The poor are forgotten with no way out:
No champion have they or political clout.

Let the poor souls manage as best they can;
Each on his own for there is no plan.
So let the strong winds blow tearing the houses down,
And the cold, flood waters fill the streets of town.

Let the poor man swim with all his might.
If he can't do that he has lost his fight.
If his house still stands and the roof is high,
He can climb as he can toward the stormy sky.

Poor man, the levees all are breaking,
Poor man, your houses all are shaking.
Abandoned, you're on your own,
Poor man, you stand alone.

Poor man, your government has forsaken.
Abandoned, your future's bleak and shaken.
Poor man, you're on your own,
Poor man, you stand alone!

Angels in April

April 19, 1995

Parents, children, friends, and neighbors:
Kindred spirits tied in labors,
Battered down by shattered sabers.

Agonizing moments standing still!
Pulverizing clouds maim and kill
Innocent people. Tragic ordeal!

Struggling through debris still flying,
Stricken victims keep on trying.
Many injured, dead, or dying.

Little babies bruised and battered,
Broken bleeding, clothing tattered,
Taken from a building shattered.

Joining hands and hearts in token:
Our nation's heart cannot be broken.
This won't be "Their" last word spoken.

We have lost; we have been cheated,
Wounded deeply, but not defeated.
"Their" undone work must be completed.

Joining hands will be our tether
For we are standing altogether.
This, as all things, we will weather.

(Murrah Building Bombing in OKC, OK)

PERFECTION
January 31, 2002

When we see the worst,
Then we know the best.
When we dream a goal,
Then we know our quest.
When we learn to live,
Then we learn to love.
When we need no war,
Then we rise above.
When we know it's wrong,
Then we choose what's right.
When we make the difference,
Then we know our might!

REVISING
November 6, 2009

I thought that I was through...
But that was not so.
I had to work more...
More revising to go.

The list of do-overs
Kept getting so long.
I wondered if ever
Could I right what was wrong!

Each task I kept working
To harmonize better
Until finally it fit
Down to the last letter.

THE GAME PLAN
September 23, 1988

The best is yet to come;
The past is what has been;
Between is what we do
To make the best within.

OUT OF THE BLUE
February 20, 1986

Out of the blue a mysterious flash tore
On November thirty of fifty four.
Streaking down earthward to crash through a roof,
Smoldering remains of meteorite proof.
Our victim, innocently napping lay,
Peacefully napping in her usual way.
Mrs. Ann Hodges was painfully jarred
Awake from her nap when something hit hard.
Nine pounds of misery remained from its flight
As it rolled to the floor and was guiltlessly quiet.

RECIPES!
November 30, 2004

What kind of food will you make today?
When your taste buds talk, what will they say?
Make something for us that will taste real sweet,
Or maybe salty or sour: just something to eat.
Make it hot; make it cold, or maybe between.
Make it good, make it great for a King or a Queen.
Look in your book of recipes rare--
Make the best of your choices a delight to prepare.

CHECKED GIFT
March 24, 2009

From the Trail of Death to our wedding day,
The rumors were heard about government pay
For the tribal lands we were forced to leave,
But never a cent did we ever receive.
And then one day it happened at last--
A check was given to pay on the past.
Not much of a check, it at least was a start
On dues for the land we were forced to depart.
Not much of a check, though it helped us to pay
For our honeymoon trip on our wedding day.

COMET CAPERS
February 1986

Comets galore that encircle the sun
Year in and year out completing their run:
Grigg-Skjellerup, Kopff, and Kohoutek,
Schaumasse, Giacobini-Zinner, and Pons-Wennecke,
Enche, Temple-2, D'Arrest, and Faye,
Great comets of 11, 43, 82, and Halley.
Glowing comets, whether evil or fair,
Wander the heavens with long, streaming hair.
A dirty snowball ablaze in the sky
Wandering from eons; ages gone by.

MARCH 20, 1961
March 20, 1961

'Tis the first day of spring,
But the cold blasts of winter still lingers
With her snowflakes still falling
From her icy cold fingers.

Snow kept falling and dancing,
Making a blanket of snow
To wrap Spring in a coat of white
And everything else below.

Frozen, snow-covered statues,
Formed from snow-laden flowers,
Stood in their blanket of snow
Waiting for welcoming showers.

THE WORTH OF THINGS
October 13-14, 2012

We never know how good things are
Until we lose the lot we've drawn.
We take too much for granted
And learn its worth when gone.

RETIREMENT
September 2004

Every day's a weekend
Once you are retired.
It takes a bit to learn it:
I guess it's just acquired.

I get to make decisions
Of what I want to do.
There are no urgent deadlines
And when I'm through, I'm through!

HIJACKED
September 2004

It was all about money.
It was all about greed.
He took all our money
And left us in need.
It was all about friendship
And a business that grew.
The friendship proved phony
And the business did too.
So we have been lied to--
Been cheated and used.
He took all that we had
With the schemes that he rused.
We have had to start over
And again to learn trust.
We have had to work harder
Even though it's unjust.
So we have been hijacked
By one deemed a friend.
As we have now learned
Your money don't lend!
So we have been hijacked
By one that is gone.
He has fled with our money,
But life will go on.

THE JAUNT

May 13, 2007

Jessica, Jenese, and Jeremy
Packed for a jaunt with a trip on a jet
To the magical kingdom isle
That they planned through the internet.

They traveled a year by its wire
For a fortnight's excursion delight
Before driving to Aunt Peggy's in Dallas
And boarding the plane for their flight.

Jessica, Jenese, and Jeremy
Checked their backpacks before boarding their plane.
With their ten-hour long flight on this jaunt,
They all slept to the British Domain.

On arriving they boarded another
To Scotland, the land to the north.
Checking bags in their first Bed and Breakfast,
Their arrangements began going forth.

They first watched a show with some falconers
Before their exploring this Edinburgh town
From castles to chapels to pubs
And to ghosts and the ghouls of renown.

With a stay at the Dairy Guest House,
To York they next traveled by train,
Exploring its castles and abbeys and towers
They found on this country terrain.

In Conwy they stayed at the Bryn
Which stood next to a castle and wall.
Though short was their stay in this
    olden Welch town,
'Twas the favorite place for them all.

Their next stay at Cardiff was shorter
And a strolling explore claimed the day.
Then they boarded the train for the city of Bath:
A Romanesque stop on their way.

They beheld the museum and the baths
That the Romans had built long ago,

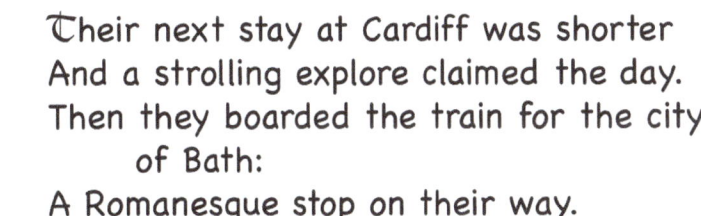

Avebury's stone circle and Stonehenge
Were the places that just stole the show.

Just getting to London would cost them the day
When travel shut down on the rails.
The landlady saved them this station dilemma
Which lengthened their pageant of tales.

In London rose Westminster Abbey
And the Tower of London to see,

A bus tour of the town and some theatre shows
Concluded the jaunt for the three.

THE PALETTE PARADE

April, 2007

The palette of colors
Begin with just three.
This triad of colors
Are its A, B, and C.
Red, yellow, and blue
Make the primary colors.
We use these three
To make all others.

The next group of colors
We can mix with just two
Of the primary colors
To make ones that are new.
This "secondary" triad
Is orange, purple, and green
Made from two primaries
And placed in between.

By mixing neighbor colors
We continue making more
New colors we can use
Than once we had before.
These primary-secondary
Colors that now we've made
Are intermediate hues added
To our palette parade.

COLORFUL TRICKS
June 7, 2004 - June 29, 2020

Have you ever had your eyes play tricks;
And seen some things that were not there?
This will give some reasons why
And these are things I'd like to share.

One evening after dark,
The moon rose oh so round,
So large, and harvest orange
Above the far horizon ground.

Why so orange and so big?
What made it look this way?
The atmosphere enlarged it
And made this grand display!

Now stare until your eyes tire,
But don't blink your eyes.
What color do you faintly see
That you can recognize?

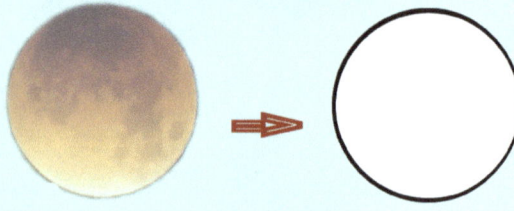

Once upon a blue moon,
It slowly changed to yellow
And sailed across the night sky;
A glowing charming fellow.

Look at the strange appearance
Of the flag so very grand,
Instead of red and white and blue,
That fluttered o're our land.

Keep staring at the banner
What colors do you see
Around the banner's glory
And faint as they can be?

For a fruity morning snack
A Granny Smith is keen.
Its taste has lots of flavor
While its very firm and green.

Now staring at the apple,
What color do you see
Around the apple's shape
And faint as it can be?

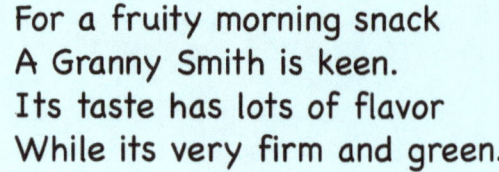

A cat named Dottie
Lay napping in the sun
And purring just to show
That this seemed more than fun.

Staring at the spots,
What color do you see
Around the spots on Dottie,
But faint as it can be?

A bird sat moping in its cage
And that was most absurd.
For this had turned to purple
All the feathers on the bird.

Staring a its feathers,
What color do you see
Around the little bird
And faint as it could be?

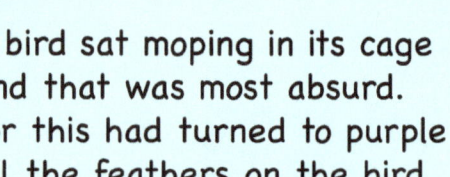

I hope that this small challenge
Showed complements of hues,
And that you too can understand
These color facts to use.

Just remember that by staring
These tricks your eyes will do
To show each color's complement
Which brightens up its hue.

Blue complements orange
As red complements green.
Yellow complements purple.
See all tertiary colors between.

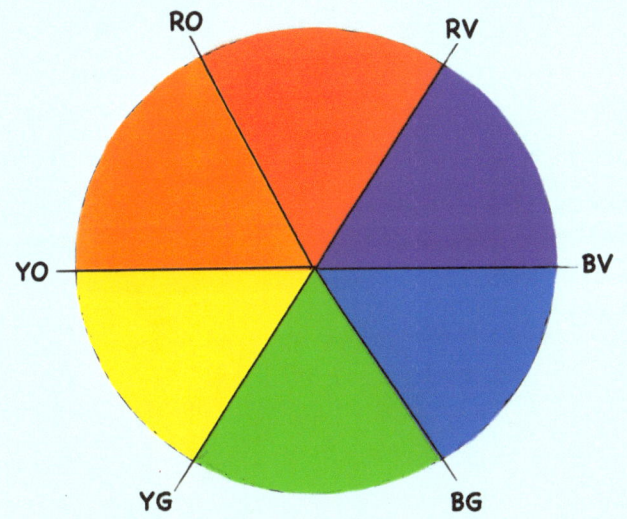

TWENTY-TWENTY
June 30, 2020

Twenty-twenty hindsight
Knows some failures and success,
Lived events and milestones;
Weathered sickness and distress.

Twenty-twenty yearwise
Great pandemic plague abound,
Faulty leaders disbelieved;
Many died the year around.

China, Europe, U.S.A.;
Other countries on the globe,
Millions sick while thousands died
After catching this microbe.

Known exposures brought about
Fourteen days of quarantine.
Wearing masks to stop its spread;
Waiting for a safe vaccine.

Many would not wear a mask
Thinking Covid just a hoax.
Once becoming sick with it
Made believers of those folks.

THE SOUL
July 2, 2020

The body forms a covering
For the soul that lies within.
This ourward, worldly presence
Manifests that seen by men.

The eyes become a mirror
Shining forth a glimpse to view
That hidden underneath its cover
To let the soul come shining through.

LIFE
March 31, 2018

While in this ride called "Life",
You take the good with bad,
And smile when you are sad.
Love what you receive
Keeping memories you've had.

Always forgive, but never forget
To learn from your mistakes.
Remember from the outset
People change and things go wrong.
But keep in "Life" your song.

SKELETON IN THE CLOSET
March 6, 2006

I know all about them;
They know nothing of me.
Alone I stand in shadow
Denied by family.

I have my daddy's face,
But not my daddy's name.
He knows not who I am
Or what I overcame.

I'm a skeleton in the closet
With real life blood and skin,
Possessing many similarities
Bequeathed from absent kin.

Now upon my death bed
A ray of hope extended.
I look upon my daddy's face
In a picture they presented.

They asked me why I did not tell
Of my existence to them,
But with my daddy's countenance
I could not squeal on him.

I'm a skeleton in the closet,
Who made my way alone,
And now as life is ending
I am to family known.

MY JESUS ISN'T A REPUBLICAN
January 31, 2008

My Jesus isn't a republican
Because he cares for the needy and poor.
He threw the greedy out of the temple
And the lepers and lame he did cure.

My Jesus isn't a republican
Because he loved his fellow men.
He spread help and salvation to all
And forgave those living in sin.

My Jesus isn't a republican
Because he helped those who needed his aid.
He fed the hungry and gave hope to a world
That was scavenged, misused, and afraid.

My Jesus isn't a republican
Who self righteously point and condemn
Those who walk to the beat of their drum
And see Him in ways different than them.

My Jesus isn't a republican
Because money and power can deprave,
By causing a lose of their purpose,
And how they are to behave.

My Jesus isn't a democrate either,
For he is above the political dyne
Where deceit and false arrogance triumph
To tramp on our laws that are fine.

MYSTERIOUS SINKHOLE
July 6, 2006

The mysterious sinkhole
In the sidewalk by the shore
Reappears and sinking suddenly
Into a hole to explore.
Once again this hole is filled;
Once again to reappear
As the mysterious sinkhole
In the sidewalk here.

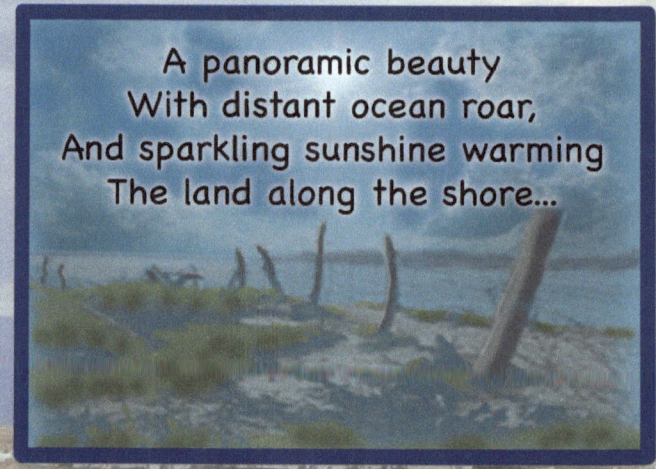

A panoramic beauty
With distant ocean roar,
And sparkling sunshine warming
The land along the shore...

DEAR WORLD
December 10, 2004

Dear World, pray for our nation.
The leaderless crony we got
Doesn't concern himself with what's needed
By changing the things he should not.

Our balance of power is gone
With the Congress held in his hand,
And the Courts are seeming no better--
His laws are ruling our land!

He's not very open minded,
And it's his way or just get lost.
With his arrogance he snubs the poorer,
And he's risen the deficit cost.

His extremism goes much further.
He favors the few just like him.
He's vetoed advances in healing,
And made life for many grow dim.

Whatever to him comes from Congress,
He signs with cameras and flair
And smirks at things far more serious
And vetoes controls on our air.

Our forests he sees only as lumber
And Alaska is only for oil;
It's his right to invade any country
If democracy is brought to its soil.

Our future now looms much darker
With this progress declining duration.
Whatever can be done to help us?
Dear World, pray for our nation!

SECRET PLACES
May 19, 2011

There are secret places;
Hidden places known by few;
A refuge for reflections
Hidden from a worldly view.

WOLVES VS. MAN
October 2, 2009

Wolves kill to survive;
Man kills for pleasure.l
Which is better?
How do we measure?

We kill the wolves
We see as vicious.
They kill to live;
Ours is suspicious!

SIN CITY
April 9, 2007

The Capitol has no honor
With only its corporate greed,
Unethical, stubborn, bullish,
With fall guys bound to bleed.
No scruples or qualms about lying;
To opposition there's a righteous blast;
If it's said enough times it's true:
Is our future a world of the past?

POLLUTED WATER
November 13, 1992

Water here and everywhere,
  But not the kind to drink.
Polluted through unthinking acts
  That pushed us to the brink.
We dumped our trash into the stream.
  We pesticized our fields.
We stripped the land of grass and trees;
  Pollution rose from mills.
Water here and everywhere.
  We never stopped to think
That might there be a time
  When we couldn't get a drink.

TESSELATED BIRDS
March 24, 1993

From tesselated words
   To asymmetric birds.
Take a square--a simple square
   And trim it just a hair.

Clip a tessel from the right.
   Snuggle it up tight
And tape it to the left
   To form a brand new cleft.

From the top--
   Think, then crop
A tessel from the square.
   Tape it to the bottom layer.

Look and think of what you got.
   Turn and twist and think a lot.
Is it this or is it that?
   Trace a line around it flat.

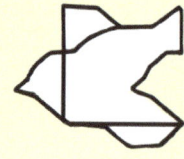

BE CEREUS
August 1, 2010

You hear of things
   that go bump in the night
When the moon is full
   of its soft, glowing light.
Some things of beauty are
   abounding there too:
The night blooming cereus
   atop Mokapu'u.

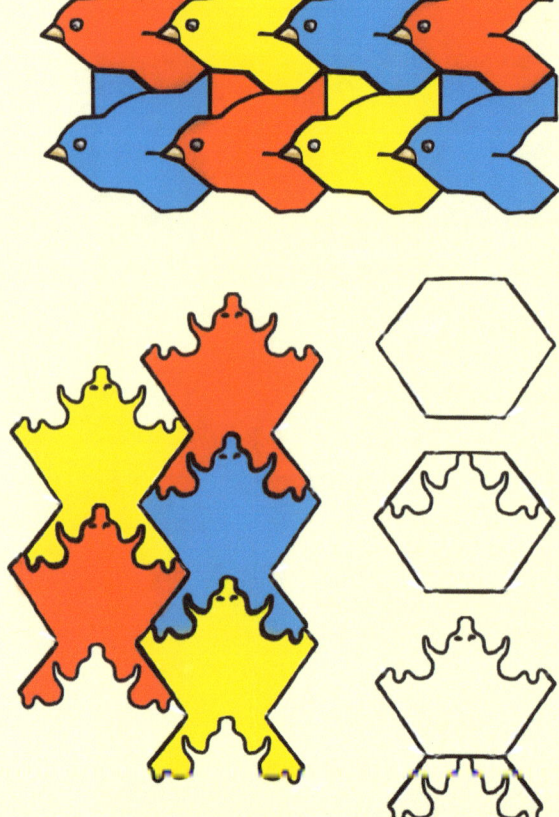

HEXADRAGON
March 24, 1993

A hexadragon isn't square
   And if he was he wouldn't care.
I wouldn't laugh, I wouldn't dare
   A hexadragon's a nightmare.

A hexadragon's quite enough
   For he thinks he's very tough.
When he's mad, he'll start to huff,
   But all in all, he's just a bluff.

When I open up my eyes,
   He decreases much in size,
And he changes his disguise
   Hexagonally to demise.

WHICH?
November 30, 2004

How many people learned to hate us today?
Is this what we call the "American Way"?
We bomb out their city,
Disrupted electricity,
And their supply of water
With rockets and mortar.
Their homes we destroyed
And their jobs where employed;
Not to mention the lives
Taken from one that survives.
Are we their liberators
Or simply the invaders?

TRAVELS
September 29, 2009

I've seen the mountain majesty
And cruised the heartland plains.
I've flown the winds in azure skies
And lived the oceans' hurricanes.
I've friends I made from distant
   parts
From travel made around this
   sphere.
I've seen the best and seen the
   worst
With memories my souvenir.

I've seen a lot; forgot a lot,
But this one thing I know:
That people still are people
Wherever I might go.
Their language may be different;
Their views may contrast too,
But when you get beneath it all,
They're just like me and you.

ELECTION DAY
November 5, 2008

The time has come,
   The time is here.
Our country's one
   Stand up and cheer!

The day is great
   Above the rest.
We've shown the world;
   We've aced the test!

For change we ballot
   That's peacefully done.
We've shown the world
   For we have won!

Hope and not fear.
   Love and not hate.
Obstacles we tackled.
   We determined our fate!

CONGRESSMEN
August 10, 2010

Some Congressmen have a big problem:
They've regressed to their 'terrible twos'.
They've forgotten their duty to country,
Saying "NO" to whatever debuts.

CORPORATE PATSY
March 10, 2005

Oh, he's driving up the price of oil
So he can get his way.
He doesn't care about the land
Or what we have to pay.
He wants just what he wants,
And he will have his say
For George and Cronies are holding hostage
The good ole U.S.A.!

TRAPPED BY FEAR
April 14, 2005

Fear is taught in the morning.
Fear is taught at night.
Fear is taught by our leaders.
Fear is our steady diet.
Fear is taught to our nation
Sensationally on the news.
We lock ourselves inside
Away from the demon that brews.

Fear is our daily shadow.
Fear's our companion at work.
Fear is ingrained in our spirit
For all of the devils that lurk.
Why do we license such fear?
Why do we allow it to be?
Why don't against it we fight,
Demanding again to be free?

UNWANTED
May 4, 2007

Life begins at the point of conception
And ends at the moment of birth,
Because no one is willing to help it:
An unwanted child with no worth.

A child that's rejected at birth,
A waif that is left to his own;
No commitment is needed or felt
By those who pro-life condone.

WASTED TREASURES
March 11, 2007

Lies for war...then
Our youth they send,
But these old men
Ne'er did defend!
Of those now dead,
Young women and men,
Could this be said...
"What might have been?"
The youth not lost
Now bear the chore...
The wasteful cost
For useless war!

ELECTED WOES
April 7, 2004

Dear Mr.. President,
I not real pleased with you
You think not of the people
But listen to a few.

You're suppose to think of your country;
Not your corporate cronies, Mr.. President.
Think of the principles on which our country
        was founded;
Think of the people that you represent.

We all make decisions and have purpose.
We all have our needs and our dreams.
We all make mistakes and are wrong
        sometimes;
But you admit nothing and council
        extremes.

Perhaps your arrogance needs to be
        checked,
And your priorities need to change..
Don't cause this nation of ours to flounder
From your consistent incompetence
        long-range.

With executive orders our freedoms you've
        dimmed
With your disdain and lack of foresight.
Remember the Russian Union fell from
        within:
Don't create for us a similar plight.

You can fool some of the people
And apparently you've fooled enough.
You've demonized your opponents and
        progress,
And your fear campaign was your bluff.

You needed a little box on your back
To tell you what to think and to say.
You've twisted some words out of context
To say things that were just not that way.

(continued)

ELECTION WOES (con'd)

You used religion to make yourself look religious
And used the radical religious right.
Your agenda is only for your own bully self
Which you mixed with your political fight.

You've told our former friends in the world
"To get lost--we will do this alone!"
What a fool you have been to do such a thing:
To squander the good will that was shown.

You're driving our nation into bankruptcy
So you can be a pal to your haves and haves more
While the rest of us struggle constantly, daily,
And our children die in your preempted war.

Social security belongs to the people
And is not a plaything for you to privatize.
Please! Not another gift to your "entitled" friends--
Please! No more of your deceit and your lies!

Our forefathers got rid of a King George.
He was arrogant and unyielding too,
And now we've gotten him once again;
He's reincarnated in you!

Hey, Mr.. President, get some advisors.
That will help us again to be strong,
And make us a leader respected worldwide
By showing we know right from wrong!

THE POWER OF ONE
June 2, 2020

One died for all
And changed the world.
One made a flag
To wave unfurled.
One marched in peace
To right a wrong.
One saw a war
And wrote a song.
One took a knee
For equality.
One found a cure
To set man free.
One looked skyward
And changed insight.
One nation made
Where states unite.
One system of justice
With equality done,
So let's celebrate
The power of one.

THE LEGACY
April 4, 2007

A world jester;
Look of a fool;
Wrong over right;
Dunce on a stool.

A world bully;
Liew like a dog;
Only his way;
Arrogrance agog.

A world terrorist
Invades and kills.
Threatens with fear.
Secrets his deals.

Worst in his stead:
Legacy tops;
Cronies or peons;
Kodaks for props.

Enemy within:
Deficits nation;
Selling of ports;
Border predation.

Sticks to his guns:
Righteously wrong;
Emperor, traitor
Knells his swan song.

CAPITOL CITY
April 9, 2007

The capitol has no honor
With only its corporate greed,
Unethical, stubborn, bullish,
With fall guys bound to bleed.
No scruples or qualms about lying.
To opposition there's a righteous
    blast.
If it's said enough times it's true.
Is our future a world of the past?

The Chronicle of 45
December 18, 2019-May 23, 2020

The top man in the land
Said the office he acquired
Gave to him the boundless power
To do as he desired.

He asked some foreign countries
For help to muddy up our vote;
To dig up dirt on rivals
That he could then promote.

He held their moneys back
Until they did just as he asked,
But then released it only
Once exposed and called to task.

Only Congress can control
Where and when the moneys go.
No one else can make such changes
Without their doing so.

His daughter and his sons
Became a part within his reign.
All used his public office
For reaping family gain.

He placed in cages helpless children
Away from parents loving care.
All had sought asylum here
To flee from dangers and despair.

So many records he had hid
Redacting by the score.
Releasing to the House
One call he made and nothing more!

He denied so many witnesses,
To go and testify.
By his official rights,
They did not need comply.

Some braver souls came forth to say
Just what they saw and what they knew.
He angrily assailed them
With raving wild review.

He did so much in open sight
Through tweets and on TV,
There saying all quite perfect
And great as it could be.

"I'm doing not a thing that's wrong.
Impeachment's nothing but a hoax,"
He whined and kept on tweeting
And blaming Dem House folks.

The eve of the impeachment
Throughout this greatest land,
So many gathered holding rallies
To clearly show and make their stand.

Then after hearing gathered facts,
The House held voting to impeach.
Their voting passed both Articles
Acknowledging his breach.

For the law's above us all,
No matter what your powers be.
The exploitation of his office
Did force impeachment number three.

The Senate next must act
To honor their sworn oath,
And choose their Country over party
Or choose to blemish both.

Before the trial began,
The Majority Leader's scoop,
"Coordinating with
The White House lawyer group!"

The House then held the articles
Until the Senate rules were set.
It took a month to do,
To know just what they'd get.

The prosecutors first
Presented in the trial.
New evidence kept coming
All along the while.

Defenders then came next,
Denying not one thing.
Declaring this a hoax…
No proof first-hand to bring.

Having this in mind, they chose
No witnesses to hear.
They voted in three days.
Acquitting out of fear?

And then revenge began
To witnesses who spoke.
He fired them from their jobs
In one destructive stroke.

Vindictiveness remained
To rear his ugly head
And smear these fearless witnesses
With hate and lies he spread.

Morality could play no part
As he must get his way.
All "enemies" he must destroy
For those "against" must pay.

The rule of law meant nothing.
The courts are his to use.
Just what he wants must happen.
It's his to do and choose.

His tweet and AG interview
Then made their danger learned.
Their cronies' sentence guidelines,
They changed or overturned.

And then he pardoned felons
Who did the things that he would do.
Although his right to pardon,
His scandal's how and who.

Since doing all these things,
Democracy has lost.
The rule of law's been lessened.
What more will be his cost?

Along then came the virus
Invisible, unseen.
So dangerous and deadly
Having neither cure nor a vaccine.

We first heard that China had it.
Soon ships found it to exist.
Next South Korea, Italy, and Spain,
Then Europe joined the list.

When striking in the U.S.A.,
He called it just a hoax.
It wasn't his responsibility
As it began to killing folks.

The states should take the steps
To stop its spread throughout,
And "It will magically disappear,"
He said," without a doubt."

The U.S. toll of death emerged
To top all other countries on the sphere.
All states must work it out themselves
Against this deadly fear.

Then many states shut down
But kept essential crew.
While some could work from home,
Some million jobs were through.

And next he practiced medicine
Prescribing cures to take.
The doctors and the pharmacies
All warned his cures were fake.

The virus ran so rampant
Throughout meat packing plants,
That mayors closed them down
To stop its spreading chance.

No showing care or empathy
He opened them all back
By the Defense Production Act
Which helped the business pack.

He bragged, "We've had a great success
From this disease world-wide
And now must bring back business."
As folks by thousands died.

He's all about himself
With no responsibility,
A lack of leadership,
And truth his casualty.

Still things go on and on
As he destroyed protocol,
His firing overseers,
And his demeaning one and all.

PRIDE
November 16, 2004

I'm proud to be an American,
But mourn some leaders' vision.
The world's too small a place
For an us and them division.

We need to solve our problems
That different views created:
To find the things that are the same
And support what's mediated.

All nations need each other
On this global earthly maize
And need respect for other cultures
That live in different ways.

It does not mean we're right,
Nor does it mean they're wrong.
It means we're all in this together
As this will make us strong.

FREEDOM IS NOT FREE!
September 16, 2012

Our precious freedom is not free
And never, ever will it be.
In annals past a price was paid
That freedom could be had and made.
But there will always come again
Some stifling act by selfish men.
We must not let their sordid deed
Impede our freedom by their greed.
The price for freedom is not free,
So guard it well...responsibly!

PATHWAYS AND MEMORIES
May 22, 2006

It's hard to let go
Or to say goodbye.
Sometimes they just go;
Sometimes they just die.
The paths that we take
Are each to our own;
Sometimes there's company,
Sometimes we're alone.
Memories are mine
To keep or to lose
Belonging to me
Or to all if I choose.

It's Time!
March 13, 2012

If we're a Christain nation:
Why are we full of hate?
Why do we lust for riches?
Why can't we tolerate?

If we proclaim we're Christian:
Are we our brothers' keepers
And love our neighbors as ourself,
Or license greedy reapers?

It's time to think about it--
To get our hearts set right,
To choose which path that we should walk--
Before our final flight.

When Jesus comes, what will He say:
We lent a hand to those in need?
We took some time to right a wrong?
We made a difference through deed?

MY PRAYER
October 9, 2007

Give me the wisdom
I need for each day
With happiness and peace
Sent also my way.
Watch over my steps
And guide with thy might.
Grant courage and strength
To do what is right.
Forgive when I err
And stray from Thy plan.
Compel me with goals
And guide with Thy hand.
Help me to treat others
With trust and respect;
To make this a world
Where good is correct.
I pray that my life
A difference will make.
Bless me and mine
On the roads that we take.
We ask for these things
From our heart once again,
While we glorify Thee
In our lives. Amen.

www.ingramcontent.com/pod-product-compliance
Lightning Source LLC
Chambersburg PA
ODITW0122101005D6
44587CB00002B/60